PLAN YOUR ESTATE BEFORE IT'S TOO LATE

900 CIRCLE 75 PARKWAY
SUITE 800
ATLANTA, GEORGIA 30339

To: Irina

My hope is that this book allows you to be more attentive, more thoughtful, and more productive.

By Brian M. Douglas

ISBN-13: 978-1540358776
ISBN-10: 1540358771

Table of Contents

Legal Disclaimer (what good would a legal book be without one?)

You are reading a book about law, written by a lawyer. There is a good chance that we don't know each other, so there is an even better chance that by you reading this book, we are not entering into an attorney-client relationship. Probably. Unless we do already have an attorney-client relationship, in which case the reading of this book will not change that. Unless you decide to fire me after reading it; which would be unfortunate, for me.

I am not a licensed lawyer in every jurisdiction in the World; so to my readers in Antarctica, please seek the advice of a local attorney for any nuances in your law. And I guess that goes for the rest of you as well.

This disclaimer is included because my lawyer told me to include it (seriously I don't have a lawyer; at least not for this book but that's an entirely different story).

If you have any questions about anything in this disclaimer, please stop reading right now and engage a lawyer to represent you before going any further.

Please note that nothing in this disclaimer is intended to be ironic, funny, or serious.

I DON'T ALWAYS
NEED A LAWYER
HARVARD BUSINESS SCHOOL
BUT WHEN I DO,
I CALL BRIAN DOUGLAS

When planning for a year, plant corn.
When planning for a decade, plant trees.
When planning for life, train and educate people.

-Chinese Proverb

Estate Planning is something that is necessary for everyone, yet so many people avoid it. This book is intended to offer the readers a means by which they can expand their knowledge and understanding of estate planning, and by doing so can remove the mystery and stigma that is commonly associated with estate planning by people. My goal for this book is to answer questions that you have and questions that you didn't even know you had.

The benefits of planning your estate are many, as I hope you will see. But if you can't see the benefits that your planning will bring to you, please think about the benefits that it will bring to your family. I have witnessed too many families experience pain and frustration that could have otherwise been avoided with some relatively basic planning, and I don't want your family to be added to that list.

What is Estate Planning and how is it Beneficial?

Estate planning is the process of anticipating and formalizing your personal wishes for the management and distribution of your assets, as well as you and your personal health care, should you no longer be able to do so yourself. By reading this concise book, you will gain knowledge in an area that most people do not think about, let alone take action on. But, by completing your own Estate Plan, you are affirming for yourself and your loved ones a task as essential as updating your family's health insurance plan or filing your tax return.

When people think of estate planning, they think about the money side of things, because that's what your estate is made up of. It's made up of your assets; this could be tangible assets like a house or your couch or your clothes, or it could be intangible, such as the money in your accounts. However, estate planning goes further than that.

Estate planning involves you, as a person. Tax professionals and CPAs deal with your taxes. Financial advisors and financial professionals deal with your money. Estate planning encompasses your finances and your taxes. It directs what happens in the event of your death, but it also directs what happens to you in the event you become incapacitated. Your Estate Plan will identify who will step in and conduct your affairs until you are able to do so again.

There are essentially three phases that you cover with estate planning. The FIRST is while you are alive and well. You can plan and strategize to maximize tax benefits, your finances and everything you want to happen to allow you to enjoy your life and the fruits of your labor.

The SECOND phase of Estate Planning is if you become incapacitated. Here you plan how everything will be dealt with if you're no longer able to take care of those things yourself, like managing your investments and paying bills. But it goes farther than that. It also addresses your health and personal care in the event that you are unable to advocate for yourself. Your plan will identify who is allowed to make medical decisions for you and how your care is going to be provided.

The most prevalent example in recent history of the need for incapacity planning was that of Terri Schiavo in Florida. She went into cardiac arrest, but due to a lack of oxygen, she suffered significant brain damage and was ultimately diagnosed as being in a persistent vegetative state, meaning there was no chance for recovery. Her controversy surrounded the differing views on what she would have wanted to happen if she were able to communicate her wishes. Her husband and legal guardian said that she would not want to be kept alive, while her parents said the exact opposite and insisted that she would not want to die.

The media coverage was nonstop. And while it seemed that it was the only thing in the news at the time, as quickly as the coverage came, it ended. But what most of us don't realize is that she lived like that for 15 years while her parents and her husband fought over what to do, all because she didn't have anything in place in the event of her incapacity.

The THIRD phase is after you pass away; what happens with your estate, what kind of legacy do you want to leave, what happens with your money, where does it go, who is in control of it and how do they get it. Does everyone just get a check and you say, "Go, have fun, do whatever you want," or is it set up with other guidelines so you know it's going to be used for education for the children or the grandchildren or for whatever is important to you because you took the time to define it in your Estate Plan.

Why do you Practice Estate Planning?

The start of every lawyer's legal career is the day they get the bar results saying that they have passed. Ironically, I received my results in the mail on October 31st, Halloween. Maybe it was a sign... It was a Friday, so I was at work. But knowing that my bar results would be coming at any time, I had paid one of the neighbor kids to go to my house and check my mailbox every day that week and call me at the office to let me know if there was an envelope. It had been such a long week that when I got the call that the envelope was there, I asked him to open it and read me the letter. The first sentence was all I needed to hear. I had passed!

I was on cloud nine for the rest of the day. It was arguably one of the best days that I had ever had, and I could not imagine that anything could upset me. Later that evening, after going out to celebrate, I returned home and my phone was ringing. It was my mother calling from California. As soon as I heard her voice, I knew something was seriously wrong. She called to tell me that my grandfather had just been diagnosed with terminal cancer. It was very severe and he had to make the decision on whether or not to attempt treatment or accept the fact that cancer was going to take his life. He ultimately decided that the cancer was severe enough that he wasn't going to subject himself to the aggressive treatment recommended by his doctor, but rather he was going to enjoy the time he had left.

What I thought was the greatest day of my life quickly turned into a sleepless night filled with sadness and shock. We laid him to rest three and a half months later.

It all happened really quickly, but I realized that despite the loss and the pain, we were really lucky; luckier than most. We got a warning! Somebody knocked on the door and said, "Hey, this is about to happen, so you need to get your affairs in order and be ready for what is about to come next." Most people don't get those kinds of warnings when something bad is about to happen to them; it just happens and they have to make the best of a bad situation. That really opened my eyes to how powerful estate planning is and how quickly life can change, whether or not you have your affairs in order.

For most people, when something serious happens to them, there is no warning; there is no "Hey, get your affairs in order" moment. You can't think that you will have that luxury and put it off. This personal experience really opened my eyes to the need to educate people and help them get their affairs in order before it's too late.

What Are the Benefits of Having an Estate Plan?

The biggest benefit to having an Estate Plan is that when you have one in place, you get the last word and therefore the ultimate say in what happens. Whatever you want to happen does happen. Your wishes are carried out and you get to make those decisions ahead of time. If you have an Estate Plan, it will be followed and your estate will be administered the way you wanted it to be.

If you don't have one, the band will march on. There are mechanisms in place that take into account people dying without a will. Every state in our country has laws in place for those who die without a will. So, your state will step in and tell your family how your estate is going to be handled. Your family will not get a say in it, and more importantly, neither do you!

And things can get really complicated from there. For a married man, assets like your house could end up being split between your wife and your minor children. What good does it do to have a minor child owning half of a house? They can't sell the house; they can't take out a loan on it; they can't do anything because they are under 18 and they are considered legally incompetent. So now that asset is tied up and you haven't done anything other than die without a will. If your wife needs that house and she needs to sell it or do something else with it, she will probably have to go to court to get permission to refinance the mortgage or sell the house.

Without an Estate Plan, you are just throwing caution to the wind and saying, "Whatever happens, happens." And as the old saying goes, "Failing to plan is planning to fail."

Think of it like driving your car every day. Most people get in a car every day and commute to work or take the kids to school or go to the store. We are in cars all the time, and everyone wears a seatbelt in the car. But why? Yes, it's the law, but is that really the reason? You wear a seatbelt because there is a remote possibility that something is going to happen, and you want to be as safe as possible. That possibility is such that you could drive your entire life without ever getting into an accident, yet you still wear your seatbelt every time you get in a car. And the reason is for that remote possibility that you could get in an accident at any time. Isn't that even more true with estate planning? No matter what you do or don't do in your life, we are all mere mortals and will face that reality one day. So why wouldn't you plan for the inevitable?

By planning, you are controlling your own destiny and that's what you really get or lose when you die with or without an Estate Plan. Dying without an Estate Plan is like driving around without your seatbelt on. You just have your fingers crossed and are hoping you don't get in an accident. It's just plain luck at that point. Some people will make it through and everything will be fine, and other people are not so lucky.

The Basic Items in an Estate Plan and What Each Does

There are three basic components to an Estate Plan that everyone should have. These are merely a starting point, but at a minimum, the Estate Plan should consist of (1) a will, (2) a financial power of attorney, and (3) a healthcare power of attorney or healthcare directive.

1. The will is the item most people are familiar with; it is the document that directs where all of your assets go when you die. It does nothing until you die, but it has all the instructions for when you're gone, including dealing with guardianship for minor children or setting up someone to handle money for minor children instead of just giving it directly to them.

   A will doesn't have to be a complicated document, although it can be; it's your way to say whatever you want to the world and to do whatever you want with your stuff when you're gone. It's the only way that you can speak after death, and that's what it is designed to do. You don't have to put only the valuable stuff in your will; you can include things that are sentimental to you or things like family heirlooms.

   The other aspects to basic estate planning cover two different components: the money and property component and your health component. Accordingly, there are two different powers of attorney to address these two components. A power of attorney allows someone to act on your behalf when you are unable to.

2. The financial power of attorney allows a designated person to deal with your finances. Unless the document restricts them, they would be able to do things like sell your real estate, sign deeds or mortgages for you, perform banking transactions, file tax returns, and access bank accounts or investment accounts. In essence, under the financial power of attorney, that person will have access to your life and be able to do anything that you would do yourself if you were able to.
3. The healthcare power of attorney, or healthcare directive, works the same way that the financial power of attorney does, but deals with you and your healthcare. If you end up in a coma and can't advocate for your own care, the healthcare power of attorney allows you to appoint someone who will speak for you and authorizes them to make decisions for you. And if you so choose, it can identify your end of life wishes and whether or not you want any extraordinary lifesaving measures in certain situations.

While these three components are not the only estate planning documents available to you, they are a good starting point.

Who Are the Necessary Parties Involved in an Estate Plan?

Different people become involved throughout the Estate Plan, depending on what's happening in your life and what part of the plan is being implemented. But in the beginning, the only necessary parties are those doing the planning. Contained within a plan are a number of other roles that must be filled. They can be filled by different people, or they can all be filled by the same person.

After the actual people who are setting up the Estate Plan, the most obvious role is that of the beneficiary. This is a person, pet or charity that is given something by you through your Estate Plan. There are no limits to the number of beneficiaries a plan can have; it is completely up to the person setting up the plan and how they want to define their legacy.

The other roles that are not necessarily as obvious are that of the financial power of attorney, health care power of attorney, guardian for minor children, executor and trustee. All of those roles are important in their own way, so careful thought should be given to each. You probably don't want a financial power of attorney as someone who is always broke because he spends more than he makes. And you probably don't want someone who does not take care of himself to be the person in charge of making medical decisions for you. For each of these roles that you appoint, it is always a good idea to have a backup listed in your Estate Plan so you don't end up with a situation where someone is unable to fill the role for you and there is no one designated to step in.

Once you identify who will fill these roles, you have a decision to make; do you talk with them or include them in the planning process or not? That is a personal decision; some people bring their children or the beneficiaries into the process because they want them to be part of it. Not because they get to decide who gets what, but so they understand the scope of the planning that is being done, and to that extent, so they can better understand what role, if any, they will fill within the plan.

Whether or not you bring them into the planning process, it is always a good idea to let them know that you would like them to serve in some capacity if and when the need arises; doing this will ensure that they are comfortable with whatever you are asking them to do. It also lets them know that if something happens, they need to be proactive and step in and take the lead; not wait around for someone to call them and say something like, "Surprise, here are two kids that we need you to raise."

When you ask someone to serve an important role in your Estate Plan, even if they're not part of the planning, you definitely want to make sure that they agree to do it and understand what you expect of them.

How Long Does It Typically Take to Create an Estate Plan and What are the Steps Involved?

The length of time required to create an Estate Plan depends on the people involved. Generally, it can be done rather quickly. And in emergency situations you can put together a base level of planning in a matter of hours, although that should only be done in extraordinary situations.

You are creating an Estate Plan that is very personal to you, so it needs to be done at your pace instead of trying to get it done as quickly as possible. If you have questions or don't understand something about estate planning, find an attorney who will take the time to educate you before the planning process begins. In order to truly benefit from the planning, you have to understand your options and make your decisions only when you have a solid understanding. Many attorneys offer educational workshops for this very purpose.

Once you are ready to begin the process, you need to have what I call a "vision meeting" with your attorney. This is a high-level conversation about what type of planning makes the most sense for you and your family based on your needs and objectives.

After you clearly define your vision for your Estate Plan, you will go through the actual design of the plan. This is where you will go over all of your options, based on the information you have given the attorney and the people who you wish to include in the plan. This is where all the details are decided. And then from there, the plan can be drafted.

Once drafted, your plan needs to be signed and properly executed in order to bring it life.

How Difficult is it to Make Changes to an Estate Plan?

You can change your Estate Plan at any time; that's the good news. The level of difficulty depends on what changes you want and how well you have maintained your Estate Plan. If you have an Estate Plan that is 20 years old, it is probably going to be easier to start over with a new plan than to try to go in and make all of the changes that you want.

Of course, this is assuming that you are still alive and mentally competent. Things get complicated when someone becomes legally incompetent and there are changes that need to be made to their plan. There are different ways to handle that situation, but the best scenario that you can hope for is that the original plan was drafted in a way that it gives someone the authority to make those changes despite the person's incapacity. If that is not the case, it could very well require judicial intervention to accomplish.

What Are the Top Misconceptions People have About Estate Planning?

The biggest misconception that people have is thinking, "I'm just a normal person, I don't need a whole lot, I don't have a lot of assets. I don't need to do very much at all and it will be fine." The world we live in is ever changing and becoming more complicated every day. Gone are the days of having a single bank account, a healthy pension check every month, and your social security check. You may never make the cover of *Forbes* Magazine, but the assets you have are still going to require you to plan in ways that your parents or grandparents didn't have to.

Every year Congress makes changes to the tax code, which can have a significant effect on you and your assets. Not to mention the reality of disability and incapacity that we all face. Your plan will address those issues and how you wish to be cared for if something were to happen to you. Your health has nothing to do with the amount of money you have in the bank.

Another common misconception that people have about estate planning is the "set-it-and-forget-it" attitude, meaning, "I did it once, so it's done, and I don't have to worry about it anymore." Anyone who does their estate planning is that much better off for it, but that is not the end. Your life changes year after year, and you need to make sure your estate plan changes with you. This is not a RONCO Rotisserie Chicken Cooker that you buy from a late-night infomercial. This is your plan for your life and your legacy. You can't just do it once and hope that it will forever work the way you want it to.

Think of your Estate Plan like a house; if you buy a house and you don't touch it for 20 years (you don't mow the lawn, you don't paint, you don't clean the gutters), and you come back to your house after all that time, what does that house look like now? Your Estate Plan is no different. Over time, many things in your life have significantly changed since you did your initial estate plan. You have to maintain your plan to keep up with your life.

Another big misunderstanding surrounds the tax consequences of death. There is a federal estate tax that everyone who dies could be subject to. This is in addition to any estate taxes that your state may impose, although not all states have such a tax. In recent years, the federal estate tax exemption has risen to a rather high amount; meaning that the estate tax is not triggered unless the amount of money left to heirs exceeds the exemption amount. In the year 2016, the estate tax exemption is $5.45 million per individual. This means that you would only pay federal estate tax if you gave an heir more than $5.45 million, and the tax would be calculated on the amount in excess of $5.45 million. So, many people take the approach that they don't have that much money and therefore don't need to worry about any estate tax planning.

This approach is dangerous for a number of reasons. For one thing, Washington can change that figure at any time without asking your permission. If they were to drop the exemption amount down, your plan that did not include tax planning could potentially do you more harm than good. And at the very least, your plan would need to be redone to address tax planning; that is if it's not too late and you are actually able to change your plan.

The other danger to this approach is that the estate tax is not the only tax people face. One such tax that most everyone is familiar with is capital gains tax, which is commonly paid on the profits made through investments like real estate or stocks. Ironically, those are the very assets that make up the bulk of most peoples' estates. Planning done properly could significantly reduce, if not eliminate the capital gains tax liability on your assets.

Why do People Avoid Making an Estate Plan?

People put off estate planning for many reasons. Generally, the topic is somewhat off-putting to people. Who wants to think about death and dying and nursing homes? To most people, it's not a fun conversation to have, especially when they are the subject of it all.

The reality is that in the estate planning process you don't dwell on those topics. They are necessary conversations to have in small pieces. But the bigger stuff is trying to figure out the good that you want to come from your planning and all the benefits that you are going to have.

Another reason people put off estate planning is that they see no tangible benefit like they do from financial planning or tax planning. We've got to file and pay taxes every year, but we would like to save a little money or even get a refund. There is a tangible benefit there; you are going to get that refund, or you are going to save tax money. With financial planning, we go to see our financial advisor because they are going to make us money, right? We are going to come up with new strategies to invest our money, and we are going to see it grow and grow until we need it when we retire.

But there is not that same tangible benefit with estate planning. You don't necessarily get to see the benefits of your efforts because they may not be realized until after you're gone; they may be intangible benefits like peace of mind for you and comfort for your family when something happens to you.

People also put off estate planning when they get overwhelmed by the perceived complexity of the process and what will be required of them. There is a lot of truth in the saying, "A confused mind says NO." Most people are familiar with the words estate planning, wills, trusts, even probate, but how deep does their knowledge go? Some people will begin the process of estate planning and quickly realize that they don't know much about it. So, in addition to all the other factors that may contribute to the procrastination of their planning, now they feel like they have to learn a significant amount about estate planning to even begin to think about starting the process.

If you are thinking about estate planning, you should consider what is holding you back and try to look at it from another angle. You need to look at the benefits you will gain from getting a plan in place. Like so many things in life that we tend to avoid, it never ends up being as bad as our minds let us think it will be. And who knows, you may actually feel really good when it's all done.

What does Eventually Persuade People to do it?

So many people are ultimately motivated to do something when they have a "near miss." Something happens to someone close to them and they realize how easily that could have been them. They may have a co-worker or family member who gets injured or somebody dies. Whatever it is, they see how complicated it becomes, and then they realize how important it is to take the opportunity to do their planning now, before it's too late. Having the opportunity to see things go wrong will usually motivate people to get their plan done.

Do People Generally Involve Family Members when Making an Estate Plan?

Everyone approaches their planning in different ways. It generally comes down to the nature of the relationship between them and their family. Some people are really close with all of their children and include them in every step of the planning process. Some people are only close with one or a few of their children and may include that child but not the others. Sometimes you have one spouse who wants to make an Estate Plan but the other spouse will not, so they do their plan alone.

It's great if you are able to include your family in the process. Part of what you get from an Estate Plan is knowing that everything is going to be handled exactly how you want, whether or not they agree with your last wishes. But it also provides your family peace of mind in knowing what it is that you want, specifically regarding your health care and end of life decisions. Family members agonize over the idea of making the wrong medical decisions, but without your wishes stated in your Estate Plan, they will have to make the decisions for you. This can bring with it a lot of guilt and second guessing for a long time after you are gone.

If you have that one child who always thought they were your favorite child or who always thought you liked one of the other children better, informing them about your decisions ahead of time can avoid conflict after you are gone. Most people are very equitable when dividing assets among their children. However, some children "forget" things that mom and dad may have done for them over the years, which could be a reason why everything is not equally divided. For example, if mom and dad gave sister $50,000 for the down payment on her house, they may choose to give the other children an extra $50,000 in their estate plan. But if they don't tell sister about this and she only finds out after mom and dad are gone, she may not see how it was fair.

Is it Advisable to Check Up on your Estate Plan on a Regular or Semi-Regular Basis?

Life changes, and your plan needs to change with it. You may have people listed in your Estate Plan today who you will not want to be in there in 5 or 10 years. Today, you may be single or married without children, but that all can change very quickly. That is why it is advisable to review your plan on an annual basis in order to make sure it still represents what you want to happen.

And not only does your life change, but the lives of the people in your Estate Plan are also constantly changing. The guardians you want to raise your children today could divorce and turn into party animals 10 years from now. Would you still want them to raise your children? No, but your Estate Plan doesn't say that. The same is true with money. Someone could develop a gambling addiction; do you want that person in charge of all your assets?

The best way to protect yourself is to keep your Estate Plan current. Sitting down with your documents every year is a great way to stay on top of your plan. But if you are not someone who will do that, then commit to doing it when you have major changes in your life: marriage, divorce, birth of a child, a death in the family, you change jobs, or you move. Each of those events is significant enough to warrant a review of your Estate Plan and quite possibly an update to parts of it.

What Exactly Is an Estate Plan Audit?

An Estate Plan audit is an audit of your Estate Plan and comparison of that plan to your life at that time. But, unlike the Estate Plan review that is discussed in another section of this book, this audit is generally done with your attorney. The attorney will not only guide you through a review of your plan but will also analyze everything based on changes in state and federal law and how those changes may impact your plan. With things like taxes, the laws change every year, so it really is a good idea to meet with your attorney annually to audit your plan.

In my firm, we offer a maintenance program to our estate planning clients. This allows our clients access to us throughout the year for questions and changes to their plans in addition to an annual meeting with us to conduct this Estate Plan audit. People love the idea of maintaining their plans this way. It keeps their plans current and any changes they want, however minor, are always done. And since there is always ongoing maintenance to their plans, they don't have to sit down and redo their entire plan every few years.

Is Hiring an Attorney to Establish an Estate Plan Worth it?

Technology is great. The internet is a wonderful source of free information and ideas. Simply typing "Estate Planning" into the Google search bar will yield more than 68 million results instantly. But discounts come at a price. How do you know what is right and what is wrong? How do you know what is current? Sure, you can find forms online and download them and fill in the blanks or even use one of those online legal sites to generate documents. But that's all you are doing and paying for, document creation. You are not being counseled or given legal advice. So, you are left to make all the decisions based on your current legal knowledge.

When you work with an estate planning attorney, you get their knowledge, experience, and their specialized skill set. They know what to do and what not to do. They know how to avoid issues that you may be faced with or how to draft a particular clause to accomplish something that you want to include in your plan. They know the law! Just like an internet search is not a substitute for your doctor, an internet search or form is not a substitute for legal advice and counsel from an attorney who specializes in estate planning.

Most importantly, the larger danger with do-it-yourself estate planning is hidden in the possibility that you may make a mistake and do something really wrong. If that were to happen, how would you know? You wouldn't, until possibly when someone is sick or dies and you are referred to an attorney because the Estate Plan is not working as you thought it would. At that time, the attorney will review it and probably quickly diagnosis the problem. Unfortunately, it's most likely too late at that point to change the plan because the person may be dead or mentally incompetent.

When there is a mistake at that point, it gets really expensive to correct, if it can be corrected at all, because you are going to have to go to court to correct it. While estate planning fees may seem like a lot of money, the fact of the matter is that hiring an attorney to create your Estate Plan will be significantly less money than the cost of having to deal with mistakes through legal proceedings.

Are People Surprised when they See how Many Assets they Actually Have?

People are often surprised by going through the process and listing all of their assets. Of course, everyone knows what they own, but how often do they think about all they have accumulated? And when they do think about this, are they adding it all together or thinking about one asset or account? When you actually start looking at your assets through the planning process, you realize that you have things that have personal or family value; things that you care about that you would want to leave to somebody.

Most people start the conversation the same way by saying, "I'm just a normal person and I don't have much." But the funny thing is that everyone seems to feel that same way; that they are just a normal person, even if they have acquired a lot of wealth.

What Happens If you have Minor Children that you didn't Plan for, Should Something Happen to both you and your Spouse?

The birth of a child is one of the most obvious times to update your Estate Plan. If something happens to you and your spouse, you want to have a plan in place for your children to be brought up in the way that you choose.

If you don't have any plan in place, things may not work out how you would have liked. Someone will have to be the legal guardian for the children. But who? You haven't designated anyone. And even if you talked to a friend or a relative and told them that they would be your choice to raise your children, there is no evidence of that, and there is nothing stopping another relative from going to court and asking the judge to make them the guardian. This could ultimately turn into a legal battle over your children.

And then there is the issue of money. Most likely, since you don't have a plan in place, whatever you and your spouse own will go directly to your minor children: your house, your cars, your 401(k), your life insurance, your bank accounts. But would you ever in your right mind give a minor child a house or a car or a pile of cash? Of course not! But that is essentially what would happen. Just to be clear, your five year old will not be handed the keys to your sports car. What will happen is that someone will be put in charge of the money and property and hold it until your children turn 18. But who? You haven't designated anyone. So will this person be a good steward of the money or will they be foolish and wasteful?

And, they are only holding these assets until your children turn 18. Then their share of the money and property is turned over to the children with no rules or instructions. I don't know about you, but I am not at all comfortable with giving an 18 year old a large sum of money without serious supervision, because as the proverb goes, "a fool and his money are soon parted."

Ultimately, someone will have to go to a court and initiate guardianship proceedings, which, in and of itself, isn't necessarily the worst thing in the world. The real problem is that your vote doesn't get counted. When you do an Estate Plan and you include guardianship instructions, now your vote counts; now there is a document that says this is what I want to happen; this is the person I want to raise my children; this is the person who I want to control the assets.

Could your Children Ever End Up as Wards of the State?

Your children could end up in state custody if you die, but in order for that to happen, there would have to be no one around who would be willing to take the children and assume responsibility. These are cases where someone doesn't have any immediate family and maybe haven't kept up with their distant family. But all of this can be avoided by naming a guardian in your Estate Plan. The guardian could be whoever you want-- it could be a close friend or family member. By legally selecting a guardian for your children, you will prevent them from becoming wards of the state.

However, the other thing you need to do is to have a conversation with that person about accepting custody. Make sure they know you want them to be the guardian. You need to know they have accepted the obligation, and they are willing to step up and do what it takes if they are called upon to raise your children.

How can Family Members Be Prevented from Fighting over Assets?

Never say never! Anything can happen. People fight over the strangest things, and with the prevalence of blended families today, there are that many more opportunities for disagreements to occur between heirs. This doesn't mean there are always disagreements; many estates are settled without incident. But there are a few thing you can do to try to avoid conflict between your heirs.

To the extent possible, you can give certain gifts to people while you are still alive. Doing this carries a number of benefits; you get the satisfaction of giving them the gift and get to see them enjoy it. You also avoid any fights over that gift after you are gone. If you give someone something while you are alive and healthy, it is hard to imagine that someone else is going to show up after you are gone and claim that the gift actually belonged to them.

Another way to avoid disputes is to involve your family in some parts of your estate planning. This doesn't mean that you need to tell them every little thing that you are doing or ask them for permission. But telling them that you have put a plan in place and informing them of the decisions that you made regarding who gets what will instantly set the expectations for everyone.

Even if you don't involve your family in the planning process, by having the plan in place, your heirs will realize what your wishes are and what's important to you and what's not. You are not going to label every spoon in your kitchen with someone's name on each. But through your planning, you are going to "label" those things that are important to you and make sure they go to the people who you want to have them.

By doing it this way, you are also able to touch people after you are gone. The loss of a loved one is obviously very emotional, but there is something really special and comforting about being gifted something by that person. It's one last opportunity to let the people around you know that you cared about them. And for the person getting the gift, it can bring a much needed sense of comfort while they are grieving. To them, the idea that you thought enough about them to include them in your planning is heartwarming.

Is There Such a Thing as an Unbreakable Will or Estate Plan?

Unbreakable, in any context, is unattainable. Anything can be broken, or fractured, or attacked with the right tools and circumstances. However, precautions can be taken to all but eliminate an Estate Plan being undone.

Every plan that is made is done so with the appearance of impropriety and is done under the assumption that the person was mentally competent. There are stories in the news where people have taken advantage of an elderly person or someone with dementia and gotten them to change their Estate Plan. Sadly, if a person gets to a certain mental state, you can probably put anything in front of them and they will sign it. Scary!

With an Estate Plan, everything that you do will be done under the umbrella that it was intentionally and knowingly done by you and that you were competent to do it. However, that doesn't stop someone from coming back later and claiming that you were incompetent or unduly influenced by someone else. This issue can be prevented by getting a letter from your doctor at the time you do your Estate Plan that says in their medical opinion, you were mentally sound and aware of your actions. You can also ask the estate planning attorney to video your planning sessions with them. If anyone were to come back and make those claims later, this video would clearly show the judge that you were in fact there by your own free will and competent to conduct your own affairs.

While those situations are rare, they do happen. And something like that could cause a plan to be reviewed or to be undone or partially undone, depending on the issue. However, this is usually not the case when someone comes in and makes an entire plan from start to finish. The problem usually occurs when grandma already has her plan and then someone comes in and convinces her to change her plan so that everything now goes to that person.

None of this is meant to discourage you, because 99.9% of the time, a plan is followed exactly as it had been intended by the person who set it up.

What is Probate and How Does it Work?

Probate is the legal process by which you administer the estate of a deceased person, who does not have a trust, through the court system. It is not an adversarial type of court case like a divorce or a criminal case; although it can seem that way at times if parties and family members fight over the estate. The estate will be opened in the probate court; the original will (if there is a will) is filed and the personal representative or executor is appointed and given authority by the court to act on behalf of the estate.

The personal representative goes through the process of marshaling the assets, paying all the creditors, and doing whatever the will says they need to do. Then, the assets are distributed according to the terms of the will, or state law if there is not a will, and the estate is closed.

One thing to note about the probate process is that it's public; meaning that the will is filed with the court and open for anyone to see. There is no privacy in the probate process. This can be a consideration as some people prefer to keep their personal matters private. This is where trust planning comes in. Trusts are private and never published, so you can accomplish the same outcome with a trust while preserving your privacy.

Why do I Want to Avoid Probate?

Having an estate go through probate has a number of drawbacks that people like to avoid. One major reason to avoid probate is the cost involved. There are legal fees; fees to the personal representative and court costs that all must be paid before the final distributions are made to your heirs. Additionally, those fees can quickly multiply if the estate owns property in different states. In that case, the executor may have to probate the estate in each state separately, according to the laws of those states. This could significantly add costs that could otherwise be avoided.

Time is another consideration. As the old saying goes, the wheels of justice turn slow. The time it takes to get an estate through probate is estimated between nine months and two years. But that time could be longer if issues arise or there are disputes among the heirs. The more practical implication of the length of time an estate is in probate, is that it means the final distributions to your heirs are held up until the estate is settled. So as long as the estate is open, your heirs may be waiting to get all or a large portion of their inheritance.

Most people like their privacy. Unfortunately, the probate process does not offer any. Probate is a public process. Your documents end up on file at the courthouse as a part of the public records. With your documents easily accessible to anyone, disgruntled heirs can easily obtain a copy and use that information to contest your will, adding more time and cost to the process.

Lastly, the probate process offers your family no control as to how much it will cost, how long it will take, and what information is made public.

Ask yourself, if something happens to you, do you want your family to be faced with decisions made in a courtroom, or do you want them to be able to make decisions in your dining room? Many people don't like the idea of a judge who has never met you or your family telling you what to do and having the ability to control what happens.

What Events Will Trigger the Personal Representative to Get Involved?

Personal representative is a term that is interchangeable with executor or administrator and is always used in the context of a will. There is pretty much only one event that will trigger the involvement of a personal representative, which is death. This will be the person who takes your will to the probate court and initiates the process and follows the instructions that you left in your will.

However, depending on what kind of planning you have, you may have established a trust instead of a will. Therefore, we would be talking about your trustee. Unlike a will which is only activated upon someone's death, a trust is in place when the person is alive as well as after they die. So, with a trust, you could be alive but incapacitated and your successor trustee would have to step in and take over.

Do Personal Representatives Get Paid?

Personal representatives are entitled to be paid for the work they perform on behalf of your estate. During the planning process, you can designate how they get paid if you so choose. Or, your state law will set the terms for their payment. Usually, state law says that they are to be paid an amount based on a percentage of the total assets in the estate.

So while they do get paid, I would not advocate a career change for anyone into the role of professional representative. Administering an estate can be a lot of work and complicated, not to mention the stresses brought to the personal representative by the grieving family members and heirs.

What Exactly Does a Personal Representative Do to Administer the Estate?

The personal representative is in charge of the entire estate. As such, there are many responsibilities assigned to them. The job of the personal representative is to administer the estate, which is commonly referred to as going through probate.

Initially, this representative needs to go to probate court with the will and open the estate. In doing so, they will be given authority by the court to access bank accounts, safe deposit boxes, and to enter the home or office of the deceased. This is because they need to begin by gathering all of the assets of the deceased and take a formal or informal inventory of everything, depending on what the court orders.

Often, people don't want their personal representative to have to do a formal inventory. In that case, a clause can be added to the estate plan that states that they are not required to perform an inventory. But even if not ordered to do so by the court or required to do so by the estate plan, it is always a good idea for the personal representative to document everything that they do on behalf of the estate. This could save a lot of trouble later on if they are faced with an unreasonable heir.

Once all of the assets are located and under the control of the personal representative, they will determine what debts the estate has and in what order they are to be paid. Depending on state law, the personal representative will have to wait a certain period of time in order to allow the creditors of the estate to come forward and make a claim against the estate.

After all of the claims have been paid, the personal representative will make the final distributions to the beneficiaries. This is where the Estate Plan comes in. These distributions are made according to the person's last wishes contained in their Estate Plan. If there is not an Estate Plan, the distributions will be done in accordance with state law, whatever that may be.

In order to pay the debts of the estate or make the final distributions, the personal representative may have to sell assets such as real estate or stocks. Depending on the nature of the assets to be sold, this can take some time to get done.

Lastly, the personal representative goes back to the probate court and closes the estate.

Beyond the probate process, the personal representative may have to ensure funeral and burial instructions are followed, and they will make sure any personal or estate tax returns are filed.

What Happens if a Personal Representative Decides Not to Do their Job?

There is no law that says that someone has to serve as personal representative. Even if they agree to be a personal representative when you do your Estate Plan, they can change their mind the next day. They can change their mind at any time without notifying you of their decision.

At that point, the estate plan becomes very important. It should list a successor to serve as personal representative, who will then be asked to serve. Should the plan not list a successor, someone will have to come forward and volunteer to be the personal representative. This person will have to go to probate court and ask the judge to appoint them as the personal representative.

What is a Trust and How Does it Work?

A trust is another estate planning tool that takes the place of a will but is more powerful than a will. A trust serves the same purpose as a will, in that it deals with the ultimate disposal of your assets when you pass away. But unlike a will that is only valid upon your death, a trust is designed for you while you are alive, as well as after you pass away. Additionally, your trust will address what is to happen in the event of your incapacity. If you only have a will and end up in a coma, you're in trouble. If you're not dead, your will cannot do anything to help you. However, if you have a trust and become incapacitated, the successor trustee named by you will step in and be in charge of the trust and your assets on your behalf.

Incapacity planning is one of the main benefits of having a trust. Another benefit of having a trust is that it keeps your estate out of probate court.

When you set up a trust, you will transfer your assets into the trust and name yourself the trustee. The trustee is the person who is in charge of the trust. So, if your trust is called "The John Doe Family Trust," then you would change your bank accounts from your name personally to "The John Doe Family Trust." The same is true with your real estate and other assets. By doing this, you are taking those assets out of your individual name and placing them inside of your trust.

The trust will contain a "rule book" that states who is in charge (trustee) and what they can or cannot do. So, as trustee, you will be in charge of the trust and all the assets in it, which happens to be all of your things that you just retitled into the name of the trust. So now, John Doe no longer owns any of those things, his trust does. And if something happens to John Doe and he ends up in the hospital and cannot serve as trustee, the "rule book" will name the successor trustee to step in and take over. Ultimately, when John Doe passes away, the "rule book" will provide instructions for the distribution of the assets in the trust. The reason that John Doe's estate does not need to go through probate is because he doesn't own anything. Once he gave everything to his trust, the trust became the legal owner of his assets. Therefore, there is nothing to probate.

What's the Difference Between Revocable and Irrevocable Trusts?

In order to understand the main difference between a revocable and irrevocable trust, you need to look no further than the name. A revocable trust means the person can put assets in, take them out, and change anything they want at any time. They have complete control over every component of the trust. Whereas, an irrevocable trust is the opposite. Once assets go into the irrevocable trust, that person has given up the right to take the assets back. However, it doesn't mean that they have given up control of the assets. If they properly set up their irrevocable trust, they can keep control over the assets and the beneficiaries. The only thing they give up is the right to take the assets back in their name personally.

Is an Irrevocable Trust Absolutely Final or Can it Be Modified?

Aside from dying, nothing is ever absolutely final! The first question to ask is why would you want to modify your irrevocable trust? Trusts can always be modified to change trustees or beneficiaries or other terms of the trust. The real reason that people want to know if they can modify their irrevocable trust is to know how hard it will be to get their assets out if they ever need or want them later.

The idea of placing assets into an irrevocable trust where you give up the right to those assets often scares people. But remember, you are the trustee and have given yourself the right to modify the trust, with the sole exception that you cannot give yourself the assets in the trust.

At first blush, this doesn't sound like much help at all, but go a little further. Let's say that your spouse is a beneficiary of the trust. Now if you need money from the trust, the rule is that you can give it to anyone except yourself. So, would your spouse qualify as someone other than you? Of course! So, if the trust allows you to give the money to your spouse, does it matter that you cannot give it to yourself? The same is true for a daughter's wedding, or a grandchild's college education. There is no rule against giving trust assets to the beneficiaries. In fact, there is no rule against adding or removing beneficiaries.

As you can see, a properly drafted irrevocable trust will give you the protection that you want while allowing you options for the management of the trust and trust assets.

Is There a Minimum Level of Assets Required to Establish a Trust?

There is no minimum net worth that is required before it makes sense to set up a trust. The real question comes down to a person's expectations and goals in their Estate Planning. Do they want to design a plan with incapacity planning built in? Do they want to avoid probate and the pitfalls that can go along with that? Do they want asset protection as a part of their plan?

The size of the person's estate may have relevance in some of the areas of the Estate Plan, but it is not at all relevant to the decision of whether or not to utilize a trust.

What Types of Assets Can a Trust Own?

Anything that you can own, your trust can own. There isn't anything you can't put into a trust, although there are sometimes things that would be a mistake to put into the trust. For example, if someone is a doctor and is doing an asset protection trust, the goal of the planning is to protect their assets from the liability they have as a doctor. In that case, you would not want to put the Ferrari they use to drive back and forth to work into the trust with the other assets you are trying to protect. The reason being, if they get into an accident and hurt someone, the trust will own the Ferrari. Therefore, they will have brought that liability right into the trust when the point of the planning was to separate the assets from the liability. A Ferrari is an expensive car and may warrant additional planning considerations, but because of the liability associated with it, it only makes sense to separate it from the other assets; otherwise, you're defeating the purpose of the trust.

Likewise, you almost never want to put qualified accounts like 401(k)s and IRAs into a trust. This is because they are specially designated accounts under the law, which are tax deferred until you take the money out. At the time you withdraw money from those accounts, you pay the tax on the distributions taken.

However, if you were to move one of those accounts into a trust, the IRS would view that as a taxable event, and you would have to pay tax on the full amount of the account. Additionally, qualified accounts also have some level of asset protection already built into them. They are special accounts under the law and therefore get special treatment from an asset protection standpoint. So, you don't have to move those into a trust in order to protect them.

The short and very obvious answer is, whatever you can own, your trust can own. But just because the trust can own it, doesn't mean it should own it. Assets need to be considered as a part of the entire estate planning scheme and not merely as the individual assets, whatever they may be.

What is the Process for Paying Debts and Distributing Assets Held in a Trust?

Unlike in probate where you have to give creditors time to come and make claims against the estate, with a trust, the successor trustee steps in and immediately takes over. Since the assets are already in the name of the trust, there is no need for the trustee to open new accounts or transfer any assets. If there are valid debts of the trust, those will be paid with trust funds according to the rules established in the trust agreement. The same is true with distributing assets.

Ultimately, the trust document itself defines what the trustee can and cannot do, such as whether the beneficiaries get the money outright or if it is to be set up in another trust for them. And since the trust documents the controls, whatever rules it sets up will define the process for paying debts and distributing assets.

What are the Top Misconceptions about Setting up Trusts?

People often think trusts are more complicated than they really are. This is because they can be longer than a standard will that they may be more familiar with. Moreover, a lot of this comes from the fact that people don't necessarily understand them. There isn't a lot of education around trusts that people are exposed to. People understand a will, at least generally, but not everyone has had exposure to trusts.

There is also a misconception about how much money you need to have before you need to set up a trust. Going back to the lack of exposure to trusts, people often associate them with the super-wealthy as a means to avoid taxes or hide assets. Therefore, they mistakenly believe that since they are not super-wealthy, a trust is not for them.

While it is true that the wealthy have been using trusts for a long time for a myriad of reasons, the amount of money you have is in no way a prerequisite for utilizing a trust as an estate planning tool.

People also think if they get a trust, they will have to file a separate tax return for the trust. In certain instances that is true, but under the common use of a trust as an estate planning tool, your taxes are not affected nor are there any other tax returns to file or ongoing costs that you will incur.

What is Asset Protection Planning?

Asset protection planning is rather intuitive; it's the realignment, redistribution and retitling of assets owned by you, your spouse or your business, in a way that protects them from creditors, predators, in-laws or outlaws. We all have sources of liability in our lives that fall under one of those categories: your spouse or children (yes you read that correctly), your business, your profession, your car, your house…the list goes on and on in the world we live in today. Through asset protection planning, there is a way to realign those assets to completely avoid having anyone reaching them. In order to protect your assets, we essentially lock them in different boxes. There are many ways to protect assets, but it will ultimately come down to the types of assets and potential liabilities that you have balanced against the level of protection that makes the most sense for you.

What is the General Rule of Asset Protection?

The general rule of asset protection is whatever you have access to, so do your creditors, predators, in-laws and outlaws.

What is the Process of Asset Protection Planning?

Asset protection planning is not much different than regular estate planning. You start by getting an overview of the assets: bank accounts, stocks, bonds, IRAs, real estate, whatever is going to be part of the plan. Then, based on those assets and the risks you are trying to avoid, you design the plan to implement the asset protection. This could be starting from scratch or taking an existing plan and either modifying it or building upon it. Then you identify who the players are: the trustees and the beneficiaries, the financial instructions, and the insurance companies. From there you set up the rules for your plan so it can be put into action.

Once everything is in place, you have to fund your plan, which you do by transferring your assets into it; that's the last component. By putting assets into the plan, they now carry the level of asset protection that you designed.

What is an Asset Protection Trust?

An asset protection trust is simply a trust with a different set of rules and a different set of guidelines than a revocable living trust or a regular estate planning trust. The asset protection trust takes your regular estate planning trust or your revocable living trust and adds to it, making it bigger and better. This protects you by adding some other provisions and features specific to the asset protection plan that you create. Basically, to get an asset protection trust, you start with a regular trust and customize it to make it better and stronger and to give it more teeth.

Why Can't I Just Transfer Assets to My Spouse or Children?

You can! And doing so will certainly protect your assets from your creditors, predators, in-laws and outlaws. Why? Because you gave all your stuff away and there is nothing to come after. But that's where this begins to backfire on you. Whoever you give your assets to will have their own list of creditors, predators, in-laws and outlaws. So the property that you entrusted them with to keep safe for you could ultimately be taken by one of their creditors to pay their own debts.

All of the assets that you protected from your own liability are now subject to someone else's liability when you do this. Everyone carries around liability; if your spouse gets into an accident, or someone slips and falls at the house, your spouse, as the homeowner, will be sued. It's the same if you transfer property to your kids. If your daughter has the assets, and she marries some guy, and they get divorced, he may be entitled to half, if not more, depending on the circumstances.

By simply transferring assets to someone else, those assets are subject to any liability that they have or incur. Even more importantly, you have no control over that person and they can do whatever they want with your assets. How do you stop your daughter or her deadbeat husband from spending all the money? Once you give it to them, it is technically a gift under the law.

So, while transferring assets to someone else may seem like an easy way to accomplish your asset protection goals, in essence, you are defeating the purpose of asset protection planning all together. And in reality, you are exposing your assets to potentially more liability, since you have no control over how people act or what they do.

What if I Already Have a Revocable Living Trust? Is that Asset Protection?

The basic rule of asset protection is, anything you can get access to, so can your creditors, predators, in-laws and outlaws. By definition, a revocable living trust is something that you can put stuff into and take stuff out of at any time you want, for any reason, which means you have access to it. They are great estate planning tools because they help you avoid probate, and there are many reasons you may want to do that. But when it comes to asset protection, you get virtually none.

Are All Asset Protection Trusts Irrevocable?

Asset protection trusts are irrevocable trusts by definition. This goes back to the general rule of asset protection; whatever you have access to, so do your creditors, predators, in-laws and outlaws. Under a revocable trust, the grantor has the option to take anything out of the trust at any time. Because they have the right to do this, they can't keep assets from a creditor. Also, a court could order them to take the assets from the revocable trust and give them to the creditor, because the rules of the revocable trust say that they are allowed to do so. By contrast, an irrevocable trust will generally have rules in it that state that the person who set up the trust cannot ever under any circumstances take the property for their benefit or for the benefit of their creditors. Therefore, because they don't have access to the assets, neither do their creditors, predators, in-laws or outlaws.

Does a Limited Liability Company Provide Asset Protection?

A limited liability company does provide a certain level of asset protection over the assets it owns. However, the primary purpose of the LLC, or really any other corporate structure, is to shield the owner of the LLC from any personal liability that could result from the commercial activities that the LLC engages in. This is referred to as <u>outward</u> protection.

Imagine the LLC is a bubble, and everything the LLC owns and all of its commercial activity is contained inside that bubble. You, as the owner of the LLC, are outside the bubble. Not only are you outside the bubble, but all of your money and real estate and assets are also outside the bubble. If something happens to the LLC, it stays within the bubble and generally cannot escape the bubble and make its way to you or your assets. So you are protected from any liability trying to get OUT of the bubble to reach you.

But if something happens to you personally, the LLC is not there to protect you and your assets. In fact, as the owner, the LLC itself is actually an asset that belongs to you and is subject to the reach of your creditors.

Compare that to the concept of inward protection.

Now imagine that you have an asset protection trust in place and think of it as a locked box. You put all of your assets inside of that box and locked them up to protect them. You are outside of the box, but all of your assets are inside. Now something happens to you personally and your creditors show up, but this time when they show up, the only thing outside of the box is you. All of your assets are locked up in your trust and are protected from any creditors trying to get IN the box to get them.

You can design a very powerful plan by combing the outward protection of an LLC with the inward protection of a trust in the same plan.

Are Certain Assets Automatically Protected?

In a word, Yes. But like so many things in the law, that is where the clarity ends and the rules and exceptions begin. Each state has its own laws in place for protecting different assets, and there are federal laws in place that protect other assets. For example, your primary residence has a certain level of protection if you were to file bankruptcy through the homestead exemption. Depending on what state you are in, this protection could be based in state law or federal law, but probably the biggest area in which people do have some built-in protection across the board is with your qualified accounts.

Qualified accounts are nothing more than accounts where the Internal Revenue Service has implemented special tax provisions regarding the taxation of the amount invested or on the growth in the account. Generally speaking, they are retirement accounts. They are accounts like: your 401(k) at work; if you're self-employed, you probably have a SEP IRA or UNI 401(k), which are the equivalent to the 401(k) that employers offer; teachers often have a 403(b) plan that operates in the same way as the other qualified accounts; and there is the ROTH IRA. Qualified accounts are protected under the law up to certain dollar values for both asset protection and bankruptcy purposes.

But, laws can change at any time so relying on them for your asset protection planning can be dangerous.

One example of that happened in June of 2014 when the United States Supreme Court decided the case of *Clark v. Rameker*. This case had begun in bankruptcy court. When someone files bankruptcy, they are allowed to keep some of their assets in order to have the opportunity to have a fresh start. These assets are said to be exempt from their creditors. In *Clark*, the issue came down to whether or not an inherited IRA (qualified account with built in asset protection under state and federal law) was exempt from creditors in a bankruptcy. The general rule is that an IRA is an exempt asset when a person files bankruptcy. But here, it was not their IRA in question but rather one that they had inherited from a parent. The Supreme Court took the case because different bankruptcy jurisdictions were handling this issue in different ways, and they wanted there to be one unifying law of the land. Their ruling was that inherited IRAs are not true IRAs within the traditional definition and were, therefore, NOT PROTECTED.

The ruling went against what many people thought, and it had an impact on a lot of planning that had been done, even on bankruptcies that were in process. So, while your or your spouse's IRA is a protected account, once someone inherits it, it's no longer protected. The one exception would be if you inherit an IRA from your spouse. The law allows spouses to roll over an IRA that they inherit from their spouse without penalty, but if an IRA is inherited from someone other than your spouse, it's no longer protected.

Why Would Someone Want to Protect their Assets?

Certain professionals have high risk jobs that subject them to liability every time they go to work. Doctors, Lawyers, CPAs, Engineers, just to name a few, are the types of profession that carry additional liability to the person for the work that they do. It comes down to malpractice. The brain surgeon goes to work every day and performs highly sensitive and risky surgeries. Just by showing up to work every day, he has an extraordinary amount of liability that maybe the guy who works in IT doesn't have. Attorneys don't necessarily have brain surgeon-type liability but certainly have a lot of liabilities because they handle property and money, are giving people advice, and making decisions for their clients. Every decision has reactions and consequences for which the attorney can be held liable.

Everyone has heard the word malpractice; attorneys, doctors, and dentists get sued for malpractice based on the work that they personally do. Not everyone has a job that carries so much risk. But whether we know it or not, everyone has other creditors, predators, in-laws and outlaws who are around us every day; your spouse is the most obvious example, even though most people don't see their spouse that way. You can end up paying the price for something your spouse does. For example, if your spouse doesn't pay their credit card bill, and they get sued, the credit card company can garnish any bank account that is in the name of your spouse. So, if it happens to be your account that has their name added to it, your money can be taken to pay the debt.

It doesn't seem as if that should happen, but I've seen it many times; you may have separate finances or separate credit cards, but suddenly, this weird thing pops up and any assets you have titled with your spouse can be garnished and those monies taken. Also, your spouse's creditors can place liens on any home that you own together, and you would have to pay the lien on behalf of your spouse.

I see this with taxes all the time; one spouse starts a business, even a small business, say a part-time realtor, and they are a 1099 independent contractor. They start making money selling houses, but they don't withhold any money for taxes and fail to pay their quarterly taxes. All of a sudden, they have a $30,000 tax bill, so the IRS and the state slaps a tax lien on them and it goes on your house or it can go against your bank account. Furthermore, you can forget about getting that tax refund you were expecting. The IRS will use that to offset the taxes owed.

Or, fast forward to when you're older and your spouse ends up needing institutionalized care (i.e. nursing home). If you don't have the money to pay for it, or you don't have long term care insurance, you're looking at a Medicaid situation where most of the assets you have collected and accumulated together are not protected and can be used to pay for your spouse's long-term care.

This means, if you have ONE MILLION DOLLARS in combined assets, you could be forced to spend more than

$800,000 of those assets for your spouse's care before Medicaid would kick in and start paying for the care. Many people will react to the fact that someone has one million dollars in assets and wants to get Medicaid benefits for their spouse. However, the point is not that they are trying to get something for free from the government; it is that they are trying to protect themselves. Because while it's great that they can pay for the cost of their spouse's care for a little while, what happens when the money runs out? The spouse in the nursing home has to get Medicaid to be able to continue to pay for their care. But what about the spouse who is not in the nursing home? They are out of money, so where will they get the money to live on?

Those are some obvious issues for asset protection attorneys, but there may be more subtle issues for people, like the possibility of one of your children getting divorced down the road. Let's face it, statistically speaking, if you have two children, one of them will get divorced. I see this all the time in my own practice. When I am talking with parents about designing their trust and ask them how they want to handle the money and property that their children inherit from them, they usually say "My kids are great; we don't need to worry about them. We can just give it to them directly, and they can decide what they want to do with it." Then I have to ask them what they think will happen if their son gets divorced from his wife and remind them that if he inherits property outright, his future ex-wife can try to take that money in a divorce. On the other hand, if they inherit through an asset protection trust that is properly structured, the ex-wife can't get the inheritance.

Another scenario is what happens if your daughter were to marry a guy who's the greatest guy on the planet, but he starts a business that ends up failing and is forced to file bankruptcy? If she inherits from you in the wrong way, it could all be lost in bankruptcy.

That conversation usually quickly changes how my clients view their children's inheritance. It's not their children that they are worried about, but their children's creditors, predators, in-laws and outlaws.

Some of the biggest threats to your assets come from places you never even see coming or that you would never think about. That's why you do asset protection planning; not only for the threats you see coming, but also for those you don't.

Do I Need to Protect My Assets if I am Not Wealthy?

Everyone has a different definition of wealthy. I have clients who meet the standard man-on-the-street definition of wealthy (meaning they have enough money that they don't have to work ever again), but they don't think they're wealthy. Even though they might have $10 million in the bank, they see people with $100 million or even $1 billion as wealthy. Richard Branson seems like he's wealthy, with a net worth of just over $5 billion, but Mark Zuckerberg, who is half his age, is worth $30 billion. It's all relative.

First, you have got to define what wealthy means to you. Personally, I don't like to use the metric of wealth because it's an arbitrary idea; I'd rather have people think about and analyze what they may be willing to lose if something happened to them. If someone has $250,000 as their life savings, they would not be considered wealthy in the world we live in today. But if losing that money would crush them, then they need to take steps to protect their assets. Conversely, although I am sure that Mark Zuckerberg would not want to lose $250,000, his life would not change if he did. This is why you should not make your decisions based on your definition of wealth. It needs to be about what you have, what's at risk, and how much you are willing to risk.

When is the Best Time to Start Asset Protection Planning?

As with most things, the sooner the better because once you have a problem and the wolves are knocking at your door (creditors trying to collect from you or trying to sue you, a loved one trying to get you into a nursing home, or a long-term care facility, etc.), it's often times too late to do much. And to the extent that you have any options, they are going to be significantly less effective and powerful than if you had implemented an asset protection plan prior to the "wolves" showing up.

Once a creditor comes after you, you have to be extremely careful if you try to protect your assets from their claims. If you do it wrong, you will subject yourself to allegations that you're trying to move assets around to avoid that creditor. This is called a fraudulent conveyance, which is a transfer of assets for the sole purpose of keeping those assets from a known creditor. Basically, if you either give away your assets (to your spouse or someone else) or hide your assets to make yourself look poor and intentionally fool creditors, the court has the jurisdiction to come and take it all away from whomever you gave it to and pay the creditor. In addition to the civil liability that you can face, in certain cases, it may also be criminal and subject you to prosecution.

In the pursuit of a fraudulent conveyance claim against you, the creditor simply has to show the court that you gave everything away, knowing that they were trying to collect from you. This is why you want to set up an asset protection plan <u>before</u> anything is happening and a creditor steps forward.

Is Asset Protection Planning Legal?

Everyone has to pay income tax. April 15th is a date that everyone knows. When you file taxes, you take deductions; maybe the standard deduction, or you may itemize your deductions and write off your mortgage interest, your mileage, and other expenses. But, you don't have to do that; you could forego the deductions that the law allows and simply pay more taxes. But who does that? No one I know.

It's the same with asset protection planning; you're not doing anything illegal. The law allows you to do it and has put a system in place with certain rules.

You don't have to do it if you don't want to; if you want to leave yourself out there, exposed, you can do that. But keep in mind; just because you do asset protection doesn't mean you don't pay your bills, and it doesn't mean that you run off a tab and you stick someone else with it; it just means you are in control now and you have options versus having someone take most of your assets if something were to happen. Through asset protection planning, you simply realign things and maintain control of your assets. You will still choose to pay your bills, creditors just can't force you; instead of following the system and the rules they create and letting them change the rules anytime they want without any say from you, you are designing your future and putting yourself in control.

You can still pay or negotiate, and you can do whatever you want with your assets because you control them and your creditors don't. Asset protection is not about doing something shady or illegal; it is about being in control of everything that's important to you and making whatever decisions you think are best. The best thing to ever happen to any of my asset protection clients is they never need to test it out! If you have all of your assets protected but your plan never gets put to the test, then you lived a pretty good life; everything worked out pretty well, you didn't get sued, you didn't end up needing long term care and Medicaid. Congratulations! You didn't have any of these issues that are associated with less-than-positive life events, and that really is a blessing.

So what's the harm? You protected yourself; you guaranteed yourself these options if those situations arose, and it didn't happen. It's like wearing a seatbelt; people don't wear seatbelts because they think they'll get into an accident, they wear them in case they get into an accident. If I get into an accident, I want to be buckled in, not because I think every time I get into my car someone is going to crash into me, or I'm going to hit a wall, but I want that protection there in the unlikely event that I actually need it.

Is Asset Protection Planning an Attempt to Control the Unknown?

Through asset protection planning, you are not trying to control the unknown; you are merely creating options for yourself if something unexpected happens. The goal with any plan should be to give you options if something bad happens that allows you to have control. If you don't plan, it's like getting on a train; there are no options on a train; there is only one set of tracks to follow. Options are more important than control. We can only control what we know and can see coming. Unfortunately, our futures are unknown, so there is really no way to control what happens.

All of us will go through significant events in our lives. Let's call it "IT." We don't know what IT is, but we know IT when IT happens. IT could be one thing, or IT could be many related or unrelated things. At a very minimum, the IT that we all will experience will be death, which is a cold hard fact of life. However, while IT could be death, IT could also be getting sued or getting Alzheimer's and ending up in a long-term care facility for 20 years; IT can be any number of things. IT's different for all of us. IT happens at different times and at different stages of our lives, which is why creating options is so important. Unless you know what will happen in your future, there is no way to plan except as broadly as possible, to give you as many options as possible. The good news is that with asset protection planning in place, you will have options and control when that IT arrives, regardless of whatever IT happens to be.

Is it Beneficial to Combine an Estate Plan with Asset Protection Planning?

Asset protection planning fits under the larger umbrella of estate planning. It is certainly beneficial to do the planning together. But it is not required. Some people don't do any asset protection planning, and some people only want to deal with the Estate Planning first and then come back later and implement asset protection planning. They may decide not to do asset protection planning, that it's a risk they're willing to take, but there is no better time to do asset protection planning than when you are setting up your Estate Plan. However, you don't have to do both at the same time. It is certainly something you can add on later. You can grow into it. If you're a young couple starting out, you might not be ready for asset protection because you haven't accumulated significant assets, so it may be premature. But you still should do your estate planning, so that in 10-15 years, you can come back and build upon your existing plan.

By taking this approach you will lay the foundation with the Estate Plan and start building it from there, so that as your life grows, you can keep building on your plan so that it grows with you. Then you will evaluate asset protection options and incorporate those into higher level planning as the years go by.

How Long Does the Asset Protection Planning Process Take?

Generally speaking, it doesn't take any longer to implement an asset protection trust than the regular estate planning process takes; you can have it completed within a very short amount of time if need be. The amount of time the process takes is relative to how many assets you have and the types of assets, as well as what it takes to fund the plan. Some people may require more than one asset protection trust, and in doing so, they may need to divide assets into different trusts, depending on what the assets are.

There is a process that has to happen, which requires some organization and due diligence as you go through it, but if you're organized, things can come together very quickly.

Can a Person Set Up an Asset Protection Trust in a State or a Country Where they Don't Reside?

There are foreign asset protection trusts and domestic asset protection trusts that can be utilized. Some states have enacted laws to allow non-residents to set up an asset protection trust there. These states have decided that they want to enact a legislative scheme that benefits individuals and allows them tools to protect their assets from creditors. They will usually have a very good trust code enacted into law, and their legislature may have decided they want the protections of their laws available to everyone, not just residents of the state. Nevada is a great example; they have some very good domestic asset protection laws, so you can set up a Nevada domestic asset protection trust if you want, regardless of whether or not you live there.

The same is true of foreign trusts. Everyone has heard about the Cayman Islands (partially thanks to Tom Cruise and his role in "The Firm"), which is where many people take their money offshore to set up a foreign asset protection trust. Like the Cayman Islands, there are many counties that have enacted laws to encourage people to move assets to financial institutions in those countries for a variety of reasons.

How Can Asset Protection Be Effective if I am Engaged in or Threatened with Litigation?

Just because you are engaged in or threatened with litigation doesn't necessarily mean transferring assets into a trust is automatically a fraudulent conveyance or fraudulent transfer. There are legitimate reasons to do asset protection, and there are certain assets that should be protected, even though you can't protect everything. Just because you're in litigation doesn't mean that you can't get any benefits from asset protection. The litigation could be frivolous, or you could ultimately win the case, and it would never become an issue. But you still get the most out of your plan when there are no wolves at the door. If you are in the middle of litigation, it's certainly worth exploring your options and worthwhile to have someone qualified and competent to help you with it so as not to accidentally get wrapped up in a fraudulent conveyance. If you are in litigation, you're ultimately in front of a judge, and the last thing they want to hear is that you purposely did something with your assets to avoid paying the other party.

If you're in litigation, it's more important than ever to try to do some asset protection planning, but you have to do it the right way and not just transfer everything to your spouse or kids. There is no asset protection planning in doing something like that, and whether or not you do it intentionally, the judge will think you did, so your rationale doesn't matter. You want to do it in a very calculated manner and do it the right way.

Will Asset Protection Planning Eliminate or Lessen My Taxes?

It can certainly do that, but the tax planning aspect should happen no matter what; asset protection should be a relatively tax neutral event, meaning it won't create taxes, but it probably really won't eliminate much either. Depending on what type of asset protection planning you do, you'll incorporate more tax planning if the situation warrants it. Ultimately, tax planning is a subset of your overall estate planning and asset protection planning. You certainly should incorporate tax planning into all of your larger planning goals, but it shouldn't be the primary focus of your planning.

RESOURCES

33 THINGS TO DO AFTER THE DEATH OF A LOVED ONE

Within first 24 hours:

1. Determine whether any of decedent's property needs to be safeguarded, such as: valuable assets, motor vehicle, and vacant home or vacant rental house. Ask: Who has keys to vehicles and properties?
2. Ensure that cremation or funeral arrangements have been made. The funeral home will order Certificates of Death from the proper state bureau or department.
3. If the obituary contains the decedent's address, or it is in the phone book and depending on where home is located, consider hiring security or off-duty police officer to watch the decedent's house while the family is at the funeral.
4. Do not to list the day and month of birth in the obituary, due to a new form of identity theft.

Within two weeks:

5. Locate the decedent's Letter of Instruction, or other final wishes.
6. Locate the original Will/Declaration of Trust/Trust Agreement and read it.

7. Locate important records: account statements, titles, deeds, and life insurance policies.
8. Make an appointment with an estate attorney to discuss the property in the estate, estate taxes, and obtain answers to your questions.
9. Contact U.S. Post Office to make changes in delivery of mail to the Personal Representative or Trustee.
10. After receiving death certificates, send photocopies to 3 credit-reporting bureaus (Equifax, Experian & TransUnion) to prevent future identity theft.
11. The state motor vehicle department should be asked to cancel the decedent's driver's license and refuse any requests for duplicates. Send a photocopy of the death certificate.
12. Order at least one death certificate for each account or major asset owned by the deceased, or at least seven death certificates from funeral home.
13. Notify life insurance companies and annuity companies of the death and request claim forms.
14. Determine if a mortgage life insurance policy exists; notify mortgage holder and mortgage insurance company of death.
15. Determine if any bills are past due or must be paid immediately. Identify a source of the decedent's funds for payment.
16. Contact any creditors who are demanding immediate payment and notify of death to make proper arrangements for handling the account.
17. Notify credit card companies of death.
18. Cancel all credit cards on which the decedent was the only signer.
19. All charge accounts should be cancelled as soon as possible after death.

20. Obtain bill for last illness from hospital doctors, labs, and nursing homes.
21. Begin to complete an inventory of the estate, list of all assets, and debts.

Within one month:

22. If the funeral home hasn't done so, notify Social Security of the death, *PLUS* any other organization paying a pension, retirement or an annuity payment. If direct deposits have been made, they may reverse that month's deposit and retrieve the money from the account.
23. Gather and organize financial documents-*including assets jointly owned*:
    a. Bank & money market accounts
    b. Mutual funds
    c. Brokerage accounts
    d. Certificates of Deposit
    e. Bond (including U.S. Savings Bonds) and Stock Certificates
    f. All promissory notes where decedent was entitled to receive payment.
    g. Titles to Motor Vehicles, Trailers and/or Mobile Homes; obtain a copy of homeowners/renters insurance (Make sure you do not cancel coverage, but keep in force all insurance until assets are sold or transferred to the beneficiaries. Some companies will not insure a vacant home beyond the current policy date).
    h. Deeds to real property
    i. Any appraisals of jewelry or other valuable personal property owned by decedent.
24. Complete an inventory of the contents of any safe deposit box.

25. Obtain the account balance on mortgages, loans, checking and savings accounts as of the date of death.
26. Bring original Will, Trust, deeds and financial documents showing recent balance and account number, death certificates, and the inventory of safe deposit box to meeting with the estate attorney. Many trusts require allocation of assets among subtrusts which is accounting and legal work. Due to Federal Estate Tax uncertainty at time of death and depending on total assets, you may have to file a DISCLAIMER to minimize taxes. Seek legal counsel for advice.
27. Notify a CPA, tax preparer, Enrolled Agent, accountant or bookkeeper of the death and the need for an inventory of estate assets. A final income tax return may be needed.

Within two to six months:

28. If automobiles are held in joint tenancy, change motor vehicle titles to reflect ownership only by the surviving joint tenant.
29. If stocks or bonds are held in joint tenancy, contact stockbroker to change records to reflect ownership by the surviving joint tenant.
30. If bank or financial accounts are in joint tenancy, leave the decedent's name on the account for at least 90 days to deposit final payments to the decedent which may be received, or to provide payment for outstanding checks which may be presented for payment after death.
31. Once the Probate Court sends Letters of Testamentary, free credit reports can be obtained from each credit bureau at www.annualcreditreport.com to verify there has been no post-death activity, as a check for identity theft.
32. Do not pay any bills for charges that appear to have been incurred as a result of identity theft. Consult with the creditor/company or an attorney.

33. In the event of identity theft, you can minimize damage by calling the police and other parties: credit card companies, bank, and the three major credit bureaus (Experian 888-397-3742, Equifax 800-685-1111, and TransUnion 800-680-7289) and notify them of the occurrence.

EXECUTOR CHECKLIST

The probate process can seem overwhelming. Most people have little, if any, experience in dealing with someone's estate. This checklist is designed to provide an overview of the most common things an executor needs to do, in chronological order.

1. Obtain a copy of the latest will. Read the will and understand the instructions provided.
2. File a petition with the court to admit the will to probate.
3. Collect all of the decedent's assets.
4. If the decedent had a safe deposit box, take possession of it and its contents.
5. Consult with banks and savings and loans in the area to find all accounts of the deceased. Also check for cash and other valuables that may be hidden around the home.
6. Transfer all securities to the executor's name and continue to collect dividends and interest on behalf of the heirs of the deceased.
7. Locate and inventory all real estate deeds, mortgages, leases, and tax information.
8. Provide immediate management for rental properties.
9. Arrange ancillary administration for out-of-state property.
10. Collect money owed the deceased and check interests in estates of other deceased persons.

11. Locate all household and personal effects and other personal property in order to inventory and protect them.
12. Collect all life insurance proceeds payable to the estate.
13. Find and safeguard all business interests, valuables, personal property, important papers, the residence, vacation homes, and other properties.
14. Inventory all assets and arrange for appraisal for items.
15. Determine liquidity needs. Assemble bookkeeping records. Review investment portfolio. Sell appropriate assets.
16. Pay valid claims against the estate. Reject improper claims and defend the estate if necessary.
17. Pay any state and federal taxes that may be due.
18. File income tax returns for the decedent and the estate.
19. Determine whether the estate qualifies for "special use valuation" under the tax laws (IRC § 2032A), the qualified family-owned business interest deduction (IRC § 2057), or deferral of estate taxes (IRC §§ 6161 or 6166).
20. If the surviving spouse is not a U.S. citizen, consider a qualified domestic trust to defer the payment of federal estate taxes.
21. File federal estate tax return and state death and/or inheritance tax return.
22. Prepare statement of all receipts and disbursements. Pay attorneys' fees and executor's fees. Assist the attorney in defending the estate, if necessary.
23. Allocate specific bequests and the remaining assets; obtain tax releases and receipts as directed by the court. Establish a testamentary trust (or "pour over" into a living trust), where appropriate. An attorney can let you know how to accomplish these goals.

ESTATE PLANNING CHECKLIST

25 Things You Can Do to Get Your Estate in Order

One of the greatest gifts you can give your family is the gift of organization. There is no doubt that your family will be grief stricken upon your passing, as the loss of a loved one is never easy. But you can spend some time today, organizing your life and estate, in order to make your passing as easy as possible on them. Here is a simplified checklist to help you get started on organizing your estate. Depending on factors in your life, there may be other items that you need to address. It's a good idea to discuss your plans with your loved ones and the executor of your will or successor trustees. If you haven't done so in a while, you should also consult with your legal, financial, and tax advisers.

ESTATE PLANNING

1. Make or update your will.
2. Make a living will.
3. Create durable powers of attorney; both financial and health-care.
4. Create a letter of instruction. This document provides a list of instructions for your survivors to follow. For example, it can spell out funeral wishes, people to contact, and where your will

and other key papers can be found. It also can provide information about your financial accounts and activities.

5. Calculate your net worth, including life insurance proceeds. If you have substantial net worth, consider talking to a tax or financial adviser to determine steps necessary to minimize or eliminate the impact of federal and state estate taxes.
6. Establish a trust: revocable, irrevocable or both.
7. Consider funeral preplanning. Preplanning can relieve stress on your survivors and give you control over the ultimate cost of your funeral. If you are a U.S. military veteran, you may want military honors at your service; contact your local funeral home or military installation to check on eligibility and availability.
8. Make arrangements for the orderly transfer of business assets. Business owners can predetermine what will happen to assets through legal agreements and life insurance on business partners.

INSURANCE PLANNING

9. Buy or update your life insurance. Life insurance provides an immediate source of cash that can be exempt from federal and state income tax (but, in general, not estate taxes). It is important to review your ownership, beneficiary, and coverage amount every two or three years to make sure your policies still reflect your needs and wishes.
10. Consider buying health/medical insurance. There are three major types of coverage that help protect and stretch your assets: Long-Term Care enables you to cover the cost of long-term health care in your home or at a long-term care facility; Major Medical protects you against the ever-rising cost of medical care; and Disability helps protect your income if you no longer can work.

11. Review your pension plan's survivor benefits. This might be a plan offered through your employer or the military's Survivor Benefit Plan (SBP). SBP choices made at retirement can be changed if you divorce or marry. Also, the government periodically offers open enrollment periods that enable the plan owner to make changes.
12. Review your IRA, 401(k), and other retirement plans for beneficiary arrangements and benefits.

ORGANIZING FINANCIAL RECORDS

NOTE: If you store any of the following information on your computer, make a list of all accounts and passwords.

13. Create a list of financial accounts. List account numbers and pertinent information about your investments, bank accounts, insurance policies (life, disability, homeowners, credit and life), and other financial matters.
14. List the location of valuable documents. Your list might include deeds, car titles, military records, birth and marriage certificates, divorce decrees and Estate Planning documents.
15. List your personal data. This can include your Social Security number, driver's license number, VA claim number, your date of birth and the names and phone numbers of family members.
16. Make arrangements for access to your safe-deposit box. In many states, safe-deposit boxes are closed upon death and are not opened until probate. Make sure <u>copies</u> of your will and other important documents are available <u>outside</u> of your safe-deposit box.
17. List loan payments. This listing should include information about credit cards, mortgages, consumer loans, and auto and personal loans.

18. List other income sources and government benefits. This includes pensions and Social Security. For information on military benefits, check with the Veteran's Administration or your nearest military installation's casualty assistance office.
19. List the location of tax records and provide contact information for your tax preparer or CPA.
20. Verify account ownership and beneficiary designations. Check financial accounts and insurance policies to make sure these conform to your Estate Plan arrangements.
21. List all organizations in which you have membership. They may provide special death benefits and should be noted for your survivors.

PERSONAL PLANNING

22. Provide a trusted family member or friend with the location of confidential or valuable items you may have put away for safekeeping.
23. Provide a family member or friend with the location of spare keys and security codes.
24. Provide easy access to your will and your durable powers of attorney. Keep signed, original copies in your home office or somewhere your family can easily locate them. The originals should be kept in a fireproof file at home or in a safe-deposit box. Also give a signed copy to your executor.
25. Provide the name of your veterinarian and care instructions for pets, if appropriate.

How to Delete Digital Assets After a Loved One Passes

By now we all know that anything that makes its way to the internet is there forever. But, there are steps that you can take to close and deactivate the social media accounts of a loved one after they pass away. Ideally, everyone will include some planning for their digital assets in their Estate Planning. I don't mean that they have to leave their Facebook account to their children in their will, but they can leave an up-to-date password list with their Estate Plan documents so their family can access their accounts, download any pictures or media that the family wants to keep, and then properly close the accounts. We have all heard of people who put all their photos on Facebook and haven't provided anyone with a password. Upon their passing, Facebook is not able to give the family access to the account, and all the photos are lost. This can be truly heartbreaking.

Here's a quick rundown of what is required by the most popular networking sites when discontinuing a social media account:

Facebook & Instagram: Facebook owns Instagram so their procedure is relatively the same for both sites. They have two options for what to do with a deceased family member's account.

- **Memorializing a profile.** This feature allows the account to be viewed but not edited (with the exception of a legacy contact allowed to make one final post, usually regarding funeral arrangements, etc.).
- **Terminating an account.** An individual can deactivate a profile by completing a "Removal Request for Deceased Person." It is necessary to provide your relationship as well as a copy of the deceased person's death certificate, birth certificate, or proof of authority for the family member handling the deactivation.

LinkedIn: There are two options for a deceased person's account.

- **How** - If you have the password of the individual, you may follow LinkedIn's instructions to simply close the account. However, if you do not, there is a process to terminate the account that requires you to provide certain information about the deceased person.
- **Who** - In LinkedIn's case, it can be any one of the following: immediate family (spouse, parent, sibling, child), extended family (grandparent, aunt, uncle, cousin), or non-family (friend, co-worker, classmate).

Twitter: Twitter will work with an estate to remove an account.

- **How** - Fax copies of the death certificate and your government-issued ID (such as a driver's license), along with a signed, notarized statement and either a link to an online obituary or a copy of the obituary from a local paper.
- **Who** - A verified immediate family member of the deceased or a person authorized to act on behalf of the estate.

Google and YouTube: Google owns YouTube, so you must reference the policies on Google's site. It provides for a number of options, including closing the account and requesting funds from the account.

- **What is needed:** To terminate a Google or YouTube account, you begin by completing a request on Google's website. Google will review the information submitted and advise you of the options for that account.
- **Who can do it:** Immediate family members and representatives.

Please keep in mind that social media sites will regularly change their policies on use and access to their site. The best practice is to keep a list of all of your accounts and passwords with your Estate Plan documents so your family can easily access each site.

Glossary of Estate Planning and Financial Terms

A

Administration – The process during which the executor or personal representative collects the decedent's assets, pays all debts and claims, and distributes the residue of the estate according to the will or the state law intestacy rules (when there is no will).

Administrator – The individual or corporate fiduciary appointed by the court to manage an estate if no executor or personal representative has been appointed or if the named executor or personal representative is unable or unwilling to serve.

Annual exclusion – The amount an individual may give annually to each of an unlimited number of recipients free of federal gift or other transfer taxes and without any IRS reporting requirements. In addition, these gifts do not use any of an individual's federal gift tax exemption amount. The annual exclusion is indexed for inflation and is $14,000 per donee for 2016. Payments made directly to providers of education or medical care services also are tax-free and do not count against the annual exclusion or gift tax exemption amounts.

Applicable exclusion amount – Another name for the estate tax exemption amount (formerly called the unified credit), which shelters a certain value of assets from the federal estate and gift tax. This amount is $5.45 million per individual and is inflation adjusted annually.

Ascertainable standard – A standard, usually relating to an individual's health, education, support, or maintenance, that defines the permissible reasons for making a distribution from a trust. Use of an ascertainable standard prevents distributions from being included in a trustee/beneficiary's gross estate for federal estate tax purposes. Depending on state law, the use of an ascertainable standard may provide less protection for a beneficiary from creditors. If the risk of a lawsuit or divorce concerns you, you should discuss distribution standards with your attorney.

Attorney-in-Fact – The person named as agent under a power of attorney to handle the financial affairs of another.

B

Beneficiary – A person who will receive the benefit of property from an estate or trust through the right to receive a bequest or to receive income or trust principal over a period of time.

C

Codicil – A formally executed document that amends the terms of a will so that a complete rewriting of the will is not necessary.

Community property – A form of ownership in certain states, known as community property states, under which property acquired during a marriage is presumed to be owned jointly. Only a small number of states are community property states, and the rules can differ significantly in these states.

Conservator – An individual or a corporate fiduciary appointed by a court to care for and manage the property of an incapacitated person, in the same way as a guardian cares for and manages the property of a minor.

D

Decedent – An individual who has died.

Descendants – An individual's children, grandchildren, and more remote persons who are related by blood or because of legal adoption. An individual's spouse, stepchildren, parents, grandparents, brothers, or sisters are not included. The term "descendants" and "issue" have the same meaning.

Disclaimer – The renunciation or refusal to accept a gift or bequest or the receipt of insurance proceeds, retirement benefits, and the like under a beneficiary designation in order to allow the property to pass to alternate takers. To be a qualified disclaimer and thereby not treated as a gift by the disclaimant (the person who makes the disclaimer), the disclaimer must be made within nine months and before the disclaimant has accepted any interest in the property in order to avoid a tax triggering event. In light of the current high gift and estate tax exemption amounts, it may be feasible in many instances to disclaim even after that time period to accomplish non-tax goals. State laws addressing disclaimer may differ, and some wills and trusts might include express provisions governing what happens to assets or interests that are disclaimed. Be certain to consider all these issues before disclaiming.

Durable power of attorney – A power of attorney that does not terminate upon the incapacity of the person making the power of attorney.

E

Estate planning – A process by which an individual designs a strategy and executes a will, trust agreement, or other documents to provide for the administration of his or her assets upon his or her incapacity or death. Tax and liquidity planning are part of this process.

Estate tax – A tax imposed on a decedent's transfer of property at death. An estate tax is to be contrasted with an inheritance tax imposed by certain states on a beneficiary's receipt of property. More than 20 states have state estate taxes that differ from the federal system, so your estate could be subject to a state estate tax even if it is not subject to a federal estate tax.

Executor – A person named in a will and appointed by the court to carry out the terms of the will and to administer the decedent's estate. May also be called a personal representative. If a female, may be referred to as the executrix.

F

Fiduciary – An individual or a bank or trust company designated to manage money or property for beneficiaries and required to exercise the standard of care set forth in the governing document under which the fiduciary acts and state law. Fiduciaries include executors and trustees.

G

Gift tax – The tax on completed lifetime transfers from one individual to or for the benefit of another (other than annual exclusion gifts and certain direct payments to providers of education and medical care) that exceed the gift tax exemption amount ($5.45 million inflation adjusted). Under the concept of portability in the tax law, if your spouse predeceased you after 2010 with remaining unused exemption (the deceased spouse unused exemption, or DSUE) and an estate tax return was filed, your exemption for gift tax purposes can be augmented by your deceased spouse's DSUE. Only the State of Connecticut imposes a separate state gift tax.

Grantor – A person, including a testator, who creates, or contributes property to, a trust. If more than one person creates or contributes property to a trust, each person is a grantor with respect to the portion of the trust property attributable to that person's contribution except to the extent another person has the power to revoke or withdraw that portion. The grantor is also sometimes referred to as the "settlor," the "trustor," or the "donor." Contrast with the use of the term "grantor trust" to imply a trust the income of which is taxed to the person considered the "grantor" for income tax purposes.

Grantor trust – A trust over which the grantor retains certain control such that the trust is disregarded for federal (and frequently state) income tax purposes, and the grantor is taxed individually on the trust's income and pays the income taxes that otherwise would be payable by the trust or its beneficiaries. Such tax payments are not treated as gifts by the grantor to the trust or its beneficiaries. Provided the grantor does not retain certain powers or benefits, such as a life estate in the trust or the power to revoke the trust, the trust will not be included in the grantor's estate for federal estate tax purposes. Contrast with the non-tax reference to a person who forms or makes gifts to a trust as the "grantor."

Gross estate – A federal estate tax concept that includes all property owned by an individual at death and certain property previously transferred by him or her that is subject to federal estate tax.

Guardian – An individual or bank or trust company appointed by a court to act for a minor or incapacitated person (the "ward"). A guardian of the person is empowered to make personal decisions for the ward. A guardian of the property (also called a "committee") manages the property of the ward.

H

Health care power of attorney – A document that appoints an individual (an "agent") to make health care decisions when the grantor of the power is incapacitated. Also referred to as a "health care proxy."

Heir – An individual entitled to a distribution of an asset or property interest under applicable state law in the absence of a will. "Heir" and "beneficiary" are not synonymous, although they may refer to the same individual in a particular case.

I

Income – The earnings from principal, such as interest, rent, and cash dividends. This is a fiduciary trust accounting concept and is not the same as taxable income for income tax purposes.

Interest of a beneficiary – The right to receive income or principal provided in the terms of a trust or will.

Intestate – When one dies without a valid will, such that the decedent's estate is distributed in accordance with a state's intestacy law.

Inventory – A list of the assets of a decedent or trust that is filed with the court.

Irrevocable trust – A trust that cannot be terminated or revoked or otherwise modified or amended by the grantor. As modern trust law continues to evolve, however, it may be possible to effect changes to irrevocable trusts through court actions or a process called decanting, which allows the assets of an existing irrevocable trust to be transferred to a new trust with different provisions.

J

Joint tenancy – An ownership arrangement in which two or more persons own property, usually with rights of survivorship.

K

No terms listed

L

Life estate – The interest in property owned by a life beneficiary (also called life tenant) with the legal right under state law to use the property for his or her lifetime, after which title fully vests in the remainderman (the person named in the deed, trust agreement, or other legal document as being the ultimate owner when the life estate ends).

Living trust – A trust created by an individual during his or her lifetime, typically as a revocable trust. Also referred to as an "inter vivos" trust, "revocable living trust" or "loving trust."

M

No terms listed

N

No terms listed

O

No terms listed

P

Personal representative – An executor or administrator of a decedent's estate.

Per stirpes – A Latin phrase meaning "per branch" and is a method for distributing property according to the family tree whereby descendants take the share their deceased ancestor would have taken if the ancestor were living. Each branch of the named person's family is to receive an equal share of the estate. If all children are living, each child would receive a share, but if a child is not living, that child's share would be divided equally among the deceased child's children.

Pour over will – A will used in conjunction with a revocable trust to pass title at death to property not transferred to the trust during lifetime.

Power of attorney – Authorization, by a written document, that one individual may act in another's place as agent or attorney-in-fact with respect to some or all legal and financial matters. The scope of authority granted is specified in the document and may be limited by statute in some states. A power of attorney terminates on the death of the person granting the power (unless "coupled with an interest") and may terminate on the subsequent disability of the person granting the power (unless the power is "durable" under the instrument or state law).

Principal – The property (such as money, stock, and real estate) contributed to or otherwise acquired by a trust to generate income and to be used for the benefit of trust beneficiaries according to the trust's terms. Also referred to as trust corpus.

Probate – The court supervised process of proving the validity of a will and distributing property under the terms of the will or in accordance with a state's intestacy law in the absence of a will.

Property – Anything that may be the subject of ownership, whether real or personal, legal or equitable, or any interest therein.

Q

No terms listed

R

Residue – The property remaining in a decedent's estate after payment of the estate's debts, taxes, and expenses and after all specific gifts of property and sums of money have been distributed as directed by the will. Also called the residuary estate.

Revocable trust – A trust created during lifetime over which the grantor reserves the right to terminate, revoke, modify, or amend.

S

S corporation – A corporation that has made a Subchapter S election to be taxed as a pass-through entity (much like a partnership). Certain trusts are permitted to be shareholders only if they make the appropriate elections.

Self-dealing – Personally benefiting from a financial transaction carried out on behalf of a trust or other entity; for example, the purchasing of an asset from a trust by the trustee unless specifically authorized by the trust instrument.

Settlor – Term frequently used for one who establishes or settles a trust. Also called a "trustor" or "grantor."

Special needs trust – Trust established for the benefit of a disabled individual that is designed to allow him or her to be eligible for government financial aid by limiting the use of trust assets for purposes other than the beneficiary's basic care.

Spendthrift provision – A trust provision restricting both voluntary and involuntary transfers of a beneficiary's interest, frequently in order to protect assets from claims of the beneficiary's creditors.

T

Tangible personal property – Property that is capable of being touched and moved, such as personal effects, furniture, jewelry, and automobiles. Tangible personal property is distinguished from intangible personal property that has no physical substance but represents something of value, such as cash, stock certificates, bonds, and insurance policies. Tangible personal property also is distinguished from real property, such as land and items permanently affixed to land, such as buildings.

Tenancy by the entirety – A joint ownership arrangement between a husband and wife, generally with respect to real property, under which the entire property passes to the survivor at the first death and while both are alive, may not be sold without the approval of both.

Tenancy in common – A co-ownership arrangement under which each owner possesses rights and ownership of an undivided interest in the property, which may be sold or transferred by gift during lifetime or at death.

Testamentary – Relating to a will or other document effective at death.

Testamentary trust – A trust established in a person's will to come into operation after the will has been probated and the assets have been distributed to it in accordance with the terms of the will.

Testator – A person who signs a will. If a female, may be referred to as the testatrix.

Transfer on death designation – A beneficiary designation for a financial account (and in some states, for real estate) that automatically passes title to the assets at death to a named individual or revocable trust without probate. Frequently referred to as a TOD (transfer on death) or POD (payable on death) designation.

Trust – An arrangement whereby property is legally owned and managed by an individual or corporate fiduciary as trustee for the benefit of another, called a beneficiary, who is the equitable owner of the property.

Trust instrument – A document, including amendments thereto, executed by a grantor that contains terms under which the trust property must be managed and distributed. Also referred to as a trust agreement or declaration of trust.

Trustee – The individual or bank or trust company designated to hold and administer trust property (also generally referred to as a "fiduciary"). The term usually includes original (initial), additional, and successor trustees. A trustee has the duty to act in the best interests of the trust and its beneficiaries and in accordance with the terms of the trust instrument. A trustee must act personally (unless delegation is expressly permitted in the trust instrument), with the exception of certain administrative functions.

U

Uniform transfers to minors act – A law enacted by some states providing a convenient means to transfer property to a minor. An adult person known as a "custodian" is designated by the donor to receive and manage property for the benefit of a minor. Although the legal age of majority in many states may be 18, the donor may authorize the custodian to hold the property until the beneficiary reaches age 21. Formerly called the Uniform Gifts to Minors Act.

No terms listed

W

Will – A writing specifying the beneficiaries who are to inherit the testator's assets and naming a representative to administer the estate and be responsible for distributing the assets to the beneficiaries.

No terms listed

No terms listed

Z

No terms listed

About the Author

Brian M. Douglas, Esq.

I have always been committed to the belief that a person's legal needs are personal and not just business. This is a cornerstone in my approach to law and how I serve my clients. In 2003, when I founded my law firm, my vision was to create an entire culture that embraced this same powerful concept.

Born and raised in Wisconsin, I received a Bachelor of Science degree from Marquette University in Milwaukee, where I studied Mechanical Engineering while working full time as a manufacturing supervisor for a Fortune 100 Corporation. Upon graduation, I attended John Marshall Law School, where I graduated *cum laude* and as class valedictorian. I was initially drawn from engineering to law because of my gifts for reasoning and logic—two qualities that are essential for a successful attorney.

Establishing my own practice has given me the freedom to take on very diverse cases over the years, which have included bankruptcy, real estate, civil/business litigation, foreclosure, criminal law, and what we are highly acclaimed for—Estate Planning and asset protection. Working in these various areas of law fits my diverse range of interests and benefits the clients we serve.

I have been a legal commentator on Fox, ABC, CBS, NBC, CNN, Fox News, and CNBC, as well as a contributor for *The Atlanta Journal Constitution, Star Tribune*, *Small Business Trendsetters*,

Worth, and *Miami Herald*. As an author, I find that I can reach even more people and educate them about life's most important legal topics. Three of my books have achieved the status of best-seller; one of which earned best-seller status in (4) countries.

I am married to a wonderful woman, Tess, who unconditionally supports me in all of my endeavors. We have three small children who make life a daily adventure, and we are passionate about animal rescue and fostering, along with all causes that help promote it. Three small Chihuahuas are also a part of the Douglas family.